SCHIZOPHRENIA ANTIDOTE

A GUIDE ON MANAGEMENT OF SCHIZOPHRENIA

BY

CELINE JOE

COPYRIGHT

Copying or reproducing this book without the author's permission is prohibited (©2025)

Table of Contents

CHAPTER 1 6
    WHAT IS SCHIZOPHRENIA 6

CHAPTER 2 25
    THE SCIENCE BEHIND SCHIZOPHRENIA 25

CHAPTER 3 45
    THE EXPERIENCE OF SCHIZOPHRENIA 45

CHAPTER 4 58
    DIAGNOSIS AND TREATMENT OPTIONS 58

CHAPTER 5 81
    LIVING WITH SCHIZOPHRENIA 81
    Coping Strategies for Daily Life with Schizophrenia 81

CHAPTER 6 101
    HOPE, RECOVERY, AND THE FUTURE 101

INTRODUCTION

Schizophrenia is one of the most complex and misunderstood mental health conditions. It is often shrouded in stigma, misrepresentation, and fear—yet, at its core, it is a deeply human experience. This book aims to unravel the realities of schizophrenia, providing a clear and compassionate exploration of its symptoms, causes, treatments, and the lived experiences of those affected.

For those diagnosed with schizophrenia, their families, and those seeking a deeper understanding, this book serves as a guide to navigating the challenges and breakthroughs in managing the condition. We will delve into the science behind schizophrenia, exploring the latest research on brain function, genetics, and environmental triggers. We will also examine the history of treatment, from the earliest misconceptions to modern therapies that offer hope and stability.

But beyond the science, this book gives a voice to those who live with schizophrenia. Through personal stories and insights from individuals, caregivers, and mental health professionals, we will shed light on the realities of daily life with this condition—the struggles, the triumphs, and the resilience of those who refuse to be defined by their diagnosis.

Schizophrenia is not a life sentence of despair. With the right support, medication, therapy, and understanding, many individuals lead fulfilling lives. By educating ourselves and others, we can help break the stigma surrounding schizophrenia and create a more compassionate world for those who experience it.

This book is for anyone seeking knowledge, understanding, or guidance on schizophrenia. Whether you are living with the condition, supporting a loved one, or simply curious, I invite you to embark on this journey with an open mind and heart. Let's challenge misconceptions, embrace empathy, and uncover the truth about schizophrenia together.

CHAPTER 1

WHAT IS SCHIZOPHRENIA

Defining Schizophrenia: Myths vs. Reality

Schizophrenia is a chronic and severe mental health disorder that affects how a person thinks, feels, and behaves. It is often misunderstood, leading to fear and misinformation that further isolate those who live with the condition. To truly understand schizophrenia, we must separate the myths from the reality.

Myth 1: Schizophrenia Means Having a "Split Personality"
Reality: One of the most common misconceptions is that schizophrenia is the same as dissociative identity disorder (DID), formerly known as multiple personality disorder. In reality, schizophrenia does not involve multiple personalities. Instead, it affects perception, cognition, and emotions,

leading to symptoms like hallucinations, delusions, and disorganized thinking.

Myth 2: People with Schizophrenia Are Violent and Dangerous
Reality: The media often portrays individuals with schizophrenia as unpredictable and violent, reinforcing harmful stereotypes. In truth, most people with schizophrenia are not violent. In fact, they are more likely to be victims of violence than perpetrators. While untreated symptoms can sometimes lead to distressing behavior, proper treatment and support greatly reduce these risks.

Myth 3: Schizophrenia Is Caused by Bad Parenting or Personal Weakness
Reality: Schizophrenia is a complex brain disorder with biological, genetic, and environmental factors contributing to its development. It is not caused by poor parenting, personal failure, or a lack of willpower. Research suggests that

abnormalities in brain chemistry, structure, and function play a significant role.

Myth 4: People with Schizophrenia Can't Live Normal Lives
Reality: While schizophrenia can be a challenging condition, many individuals manage their symptoms and lead fulfilling lives. With the right combination of medication, therapy, and social support, people with schizophrenia can work, maintain relationships, and pursue their passions. Early intervention and ongoing treatment make a significant difference in improving quality of life.

Myth 5: Schizophrenia Has No Effective Treatments
Reality: While schizophrenia is a lifelong condition, it is treatable. Antipsychotic medications, therapy, social support, and lifestyle changes help individuals manage their symptoms. Advances in research continue to improve treatment options,

offering hope for better management and recovery.

How Schizophrenia Affects Thinking, Emotions, and Perception
Schizophrenia is a disorder that deeply impacts how a person thinks, feels, and perceives the world. It disrupts normal cognitive processes, distorts emotions, and alters sensory experiences, making daily life challenging for those affected. Understanding these effects is crucial for recognizing the struggles individuals face and providing the right support.

Disruptions in Thinking
People with schizophrenia often experience disorganized thinking, which can make communication and decision-making difficult. Thoughts may become fragmented, illogical, or disconnected from reality. This can manifest in several ways:
    1. Disorganized Speech – A person may struggle to form coherent sentences,

jumping from one topic to another in a way that is hard to follow.
2. Delusions – Strongly held false beliefs that persist despite evidence to the contrary. For example, a person may believe they are being watched, controlled, or given special powers.
3. Impaired Memory and Concentration – Difficulty focusing, remembering details, or following conversations can affect work, relationships, and daily tasks.

Emotional Disturbances

Schizophrenia can also affect emotional responses, making it difficult for individuals to express or even feel emotions in typical ways. This may include:
- Blunted Affect – Reduced ability to show emotions through facial expressions, tone of voice, or body language. A person might seem emotionally detached or indifferent,

even in situations that typically provoke strong feelings.
- Inappropriate Emotional Responses – Some individuals may react in ways that seem out of place, such as laughing at sad news or becoming upset over minor issues.
- Anhedonia – A reduced ability to feel pleasure, leading to a loss of interest in activities or relationships that once brought joy.

Altered Perception
One of the most profound effects of schizophrenia is the way it distorts perception. This can include:
- Hallucinations – The most common are auditory hallucinations, where a person hears voices that others do not. These voices may be critical, commanding, or conversational. Some individuals also experience visual, tactile, or olfactory hallucinations.

- Derealization – The world may feel unreal or distorted, as if the person is watching life through a fog or a screen.
- Changes in Sensory Processing – Some people become overly sensitive to sounds, lights, or touch, while others may feel disconnected from their environment.

The Impact on Daily Life
These cognitive, emotional, and perceptual disturbances can make everyday life challenging. Maintaining relationships, holding a job, or even completing basic tasks can require significant effort. However, with treatment, therapy, and support, many individuals with schizophrenia learn to manage their symptoms and lead fulfilling lives.

Understanding these effects helps reduce stigma and encourages a more compassionate approach to supporting those with schizophrenia. Rather than viewing the condition as a mystery or a source of fear, recognizing it as a complex but treatable disorder allows for greater empathy and effective care.

Common Symptoms of Schizophrenia: Hallucinations, Delusions, and Disorganized Thinking

Schizophrenia is a complex mental disorder characterized by a range of symptoms that affect perception, thought processes, and behavior. Among the most prominent symptoms are hallucinations, delusions, and disorganized thinking. These symptoms can be distressing and significantly impact a person's ability to function in daily life.

Hallucinations
Hallucinations are sensory experiences that occur without any external stimulus. They can affect any of the five senses, but *auditory hallucinations—hearing voices—are the most common in schizophrenia.

- Auditory Hallucinations: A person may hear voices speaking to them, commenting on their actions, or even arguing with one another. These voices can be friendly, neutral, or distressing, and in some cases, they may command the person to do things.
- Visual Hallucinations: Some individuals see things that are not there, such as people, shapes, or lights.
- Tactile Hallucinations: A person might feel sensations like bugs crawling on their skin or an unseen force touching them.
- Olfactory and Gustatory Hallucinations: Some may smell or taste things that others do not, which can contribute to paranoia, such as believing food is poisoned.

Hallucinations feel very real to the person experiencing them, making it difficult for them to distinguish between their perceptions and reality.

Delusions
Delusions are strongly held false beliefs that persist despite clear evidence to the contrary. They often revolve around themes of persecution, grandiosity, or control.
- Paranoid Delusions: The belief that others are spying on, plotting against, or trying to harm them. For example, a person may think that the government or a neighbor is tracking their movements.
- Delusions of Grandeur: The belief that one has exceptional abilities, fame, or a special connection to a higher power. A person might believe they are a famous historical figure or have been chosen to complete an important mission.
- Delusions of Control: The belief that external forces, such as aliens, the government, or supernatural entities,

are controlling their thoughts, actions, or body.
- Somatic Delusions: False beliefs about bodily functions or sensations, such as believing that organs have been removed or that parasites are living inside the body.

Delusions can cause distress and influence behavior in ways that make daily life challenging.

Disorganized Thinking
Disorganized thinking affects a person's ability to organize thoughts, follow conversations, and express themselves clearly. This can make communication difficult and lead to misunderstandings.
- Disorganized Speech: A person may jump from one topic to another without logical connections, use made-up words, or speak in a way that is difficult to understand.
- Trouble Concentrating: Individuals may find it hard to focus on tasks,

follow instructions, or remember details.
- Difficulty Planning and Organizing: Simple activities, like preparing a meal or following a daily routine, may become overwhelming due to scattered thoughts.

In severe cases, disorganized thinking can lead to word salad (a jumble of unrelated words) or thought blocking, where a person suddenly stops speaking mid-sentence, as if the thought has vanished.

The Impact of These Symptoms
Hallucinations, delusions, and disorganized thinking can make it difficult for individuals with schizophrenia to distinguish reality from their internal experiences. This can lead to social withdrawal, difficulty maintaining relationships, and struggles with employment or daily responsibilities. However, with the right treatment—including medication, therapy, and support—many people with schizophrenia can manage their

symptoms and lead meaningful lives. Understanding these symptoms is key to reducing stigma and offering the right support to those affected by the disorder.

Different Types of Schizophrenia and Related Disorders

Schizophrenia is a complex mental health disorder, but it does not present the same way in every individual. Historically, schizophrenia was categorized into subtypes, such as paranoid, disorganized, and catatonic schizophrenia. However, modern diagnostic systems like the DSM-5 (Diagnostic and Statistical Manual of Mental Disorders, 5th Edition) have moved away from these subtypes, recognizing that schizophrenia exists on a spectrum with overlapping symptoms. Instead, schizophrenia is now considered part of a broader category of schizophrenia spectrum and related disorders.

Below are the different types of schizophrenia-related disorders and their unique characteristics:

1. Schizophrenia
Schizophrenia is the primary disorder within this spectrum, characterized by:
- Hallucinations (most commonly auditory, such as hearing voices)
- Delusions (false, strongly held beliefs)
- Disorganized thinking and speech
- Severe difficulty in functioning (socially, occupationally, and personally)

Symptoms must persist for at least six months to be diagnosed as schizophrenia.

2. Schizoaffective Disorder

Schizoaffective disorder is a combination of schizophrenia and mood disorders (such as bipolar disorder or major depression). People with schizoaffective disorder experience:

- Psychotic symptoms (hallucinations and delusions)
- Mood episodes (either major depression or mania)
- Periods of psychosis without mood symptoms

This condition is often misdiagnosed as either schizophrenia or bipolar disorder, but it requires distinct treatment approaches.

3. Schizophreniform Disorder

This disorder shares the same symptoms as schizophrenia but lasts for a shorter duration—between one and six months. If symptoms persist beyond six months, the diagnosis may be updated to schizophrenia. Some individuals with schizophreniform disorder recover fully, while others go on to develop chronic schizophrenia.

4. Brief Psychotic Disorder

This condition involves a sudden and temporary episode of psychosis, including hallucinations, delusions, or disorganized speech. Unlike schizophrenia, symptoms last between one day and one month and often resolve completely.It may be triggered by extreme stress, trauma, or postpartum changes in women.Some individuals never experience another episode, while others may later develop schizophrenia.

5. Delusional Disorder
Individuals with delusional disorder experience persistent delusions (false beliefs) but generally do not have the other symptoms of schizophrenia (such as hallucinations or disorganized thinking). The delusions often involve:
- Persecution (paranoid delusions) – believing they are being followed, spied on, or conspired against.
- Grandiosity – believing they have special powers, knowledge, or a relationship with famous figures.
- Jealousy – believing a partner is unfaithful despite lack of evidence.

- Somatic delusions – believing they have a serious but undiagnosed medical condition.

Unlike schizophrenia, people with delusional disorder can often function in daily life but may struggle socially due to their rigid belief system.

6. Catatonia (Schizophrenia with Catatonic Features)

Catatonia is a condition that can occur in schizophrenia or other mental disorders. It involves abnormal movement and behavior, such as:

- Stupor – being unresponsive or unable to move for long periods.
- Mutism – not speaking despite being physically able to.
- Waxy flexibility – maintaining an unusual posture when placed in one by someone else.
- Agitation – sudden, purposeless movements or extreme restlessness.

Catatonia was previously considered a distinct type of schizophrenia but is now classified as a specifier that can occur in various disorders.

7. Psychotic Disorder Due to a Medical Condition or Substance Use
Psychotic symptoms similar to schizophrenia can occur due to:
- Substance-induced psychosis – caused by drug use (e.g., hallucinogens, amphetamines, or alcohol withdrawal).
- Medical conditions – such as brain injuries, tumors, or neurological disorders (e.g., Parkinson's disease, epilepsy).
- Dementia-related psychosis – seen in Alzheimer's or Lewy body dementia.

Treatment focuses on addressing the underlying cause rather than treating it as schizophrenia.

Understanding the Spectrum

Schizophrenia and related disorders exist on a spectrum, meaning symptoms can overlap and vary in severity. While schizophrenia is a lifelong condition requiring long-term treatment, some related disorders, like brief psychotic disorder or schizophreniform disorder, may resolve completely with proper care.

By recognizing the different types of schizophrenia-related conditions, we can better understand their complexities and provide appropriate support and treatment for those affected.

CHAPTER 2

THE SCIENCE BEHIND SCHIZOPHRENIA

What Causes Schizophrenia? The Role of Genetics and Brain Chemistry

Schizophrenia is a complex mental disorder with no single cause. Instead, it arises from a combination of genetic, biological, and environmental factors that influence brain function. While the exact cause remains unknown, research suggests that genetics and brain chemistry play significant roles in its development.

The Role of Genetics

Schizophrenia tends to run in families, suggesting a strong genetic component. However, it is not caused by a single gene but rather by a combination of multiple genes interacting with environmental factors.

- Family History and Risk – A person with a close relative (such as a parent or sibling) with schizophrenia has a higher risk of developing the disorder.
- Twin Studies – Identical twins, who share 100% of their genes, have a 40–50% chance of both developing schizophrenia if one twin is affected. However, since this is not 100%, genetics alone do not fully determine the disorder.
- Gene Variations – Researchers have identified several genes associated with schizophrenia, particularly those involved in brain development, neurotransmitter function, and immune system regulation.

While genetics increase the likelihood of developing schizophrenia, they do not guarantee it. Environmental factors often play a crucial role in triggering the disorder in those who are genetically predisposed.

Brain Chemistry and Neurotransmitters

Schizophrenia is linked to imbalances in brain chemicals, particularly neurotransmitters that regulate thoughts, emotions, and perception.

- Dopamine Dysfunction – The most widely accepted theory suggests that schizophrenia involves an overactivity of dopamine in certain brain regions. Excess dopamine in the limbic system is believed to contribute to hallucinations and delusions. Low dopamine in the prefrontal cortex may lead to cognitive difficulties and negative symptoms, such as reduced motivation and emotional expression.
- Glutamate Dysfunction – Glutamate, another important neurotransmitter, is also thought to play a role. Studies suggest that low glutamate activity in the brain may contribute to schizophrenia symptoms, particularly cognitive impairments.

- Serotonin Involvement – Some research indicates that serotonin imbalances may contribute to mood disturbances and psychotic symptoms in schizophrenia. This is why some antipsychotic medications target both dopamine and serotonin receptors.

Brain Structure and Function
Studies using brain imaging techniques have shown that individuals with schizophrenia often have differences in brain structure and function, including:
- Enlarged Ventricles – The fluid-filled spaces in the brain (ventricles) are often larger in people with schizophrenia, suggesting a loss of brain tissue.
- Reduced Gray Matter – Some areas of the brain, particularly the prefrontal cortex (responsible for reasoning and decision-making), may have less gray matter, leading to cognitive and emotional difficulties.

- Abnormal Connectivity – Disruptions in communication between different brain regions may contribute to the disorder's symptoms.

The Interaction of Genetics and Brain Chemistry

While genetics create a predisposition for schizophrenia, it is the combination of genetic vulnerability and brain chemistry imbalances that ultimately leads to the disorder. Additionally, environmental factors, such as prenatal complications, stress, or substance use, may act as triggers that bring out the symptoms in those who are already at risk.

Understanding the biological causes of schizophrenia is essential for developing better treatments. Current research continues to explore how genetic factors, brain chemistry, and neural pathways interact to cause this complex disorder.

How the Brain Processes Reality Differently in Schizophrenia

Schizophrenia fundamentally alters the way the brain interprets reality, leading to hallucinations, delusions, and disorganized thinking. These distortions are not simply a matter of perception but are rooted in neurobiological changes that affect how information is processed. To understand how schizophrenia affects reality perception, we need to examine how the brain normally constructs reality and how this process is disrupted in individuals with schizophrenia.

1. Perception and Sensory Processing
The human brain constantly filters and interprets sensory information from the environment. Normally, it organizes these inputs into a coherent picture of reality. However, in schizophrenia, this filtering system is impaired, leading to sensory overload or distorted perceptions.Hallucinations (especially auditory hallucinations) occur because the

brain misidentifies internal thoughts or background noise as external stimuli.Dopamine overactivity in the brain's sensory processing centers, like the thalamus, can cause false sensory experiences, making hallucinations seem real.Reduced sensory gating (the brain's ability to ignore irrelevant stimuli) leads to an overwhelming flood of sensory information, making it difficult to focus on reality.

2. Thought Processing and Reality Distortion
Schizophrenia disrupts thought organization, making it harder to separate real events from imagined ones.Disorganized thinking results from abnormal connectivity between brain regions that regulate thought processes. This can cause random associations between unrelated ideas, leading to illogical conclusions or fragmented speech.Delusions arise because of faulty

reasoning and misinterpretation of experiences. The brain mistakenly assigns excessive importance to random thoughts, leading to false beliefs, such as paranoia or grandiosity. Hyperactive dopamine signaling in the striatum may cause heightened salience—where insignificant details feel extremely important—fueling delusions.

3. Memory and Self-Awareness
Memory plays a crucial role in distinguishing real experiences from imagined ones. In schizophrenia, memory distortions and reduced self-awareness contribute to reality confusion.

- Source monitoring deficits – People with schizophrenia may struggle to determine whether a memory is real or imagined, leading to false recollections or fabricated experiences.
- Reduced connectivity in the default mode network (DMN) – This brain network is responsible for self-

reflection and distinguishing between internal thoughts and external reality. In schizophrenia, this system is impaired, making it difficult to differentiate between self-generated thoughts and actual events.
Confusion between dreams and reality – Some individuals may recall dreams, intrusive thoughts, or daydreams as real-life events.

4. Emotional Perception and Social Reality
Emotions help shape our understanding of social interactions and reality.
Schizophrenia disrupts emotional regulation, making it difficult to interpret facial expressions, tone of voice, and social cues.
- Blunted affect – Reduced emotional responsiveness can make individuals appear indifferent or disconnected from reality.
- Paranoia and misinterpretation of others' intentions – Social cues are

often misread, leading to increased distrust or fear in social interactions.
- Altered amygdala activity – The amygdala, responsible for processing emotions, may overreact to neutral expressions, making them seem threatening.

5. Predictive Processing and Expectation Errors

The brain constantly predicts future events based on past experiences. In schizophrenia, these predictions become unreliable, leading to unexpected interpretations of reality.

The brain over-predicts or misattributed causes to events, leading to delusions of control or paranoia.

Sensory inputs that don't match expectations may be interpreted as threats (e.g., hearing a stranger laugh and believing they are mocking you).

Abnormal dopamine release may cause excessive pattern recognition, making people see meaningful connections where none exist (e.g., believing unrelated events are part of a conspiracy).

Environmental Triggers: Stress, Trauma, and Substance Use

While genetics and brain chemistry play a significant role in schizophrenia, environmental factors can act as triggers that bring out symptoms in individuals who are already vulnerable. Among these, stress, trauma, and substance use are some of the most well-documented influences that can contribute to the onset or worsening of the disorder.

1. Stress as a Trigger

Stress does not directly cause schizophrenia, but it can exacerbate symptoms or trigger an episode in someone who is already predisposed to the disorder. The brain's stress response system, particularly the hypothalamic-pituitary-adrenal (HPA) axis, becomes overactive in schizophrenia, making individuals more sensitive to stress.

- Major life changes – Events such as moving to a new city, starting a new job, or the loss of a loved one can contribute to the onset of symptoms.
- Social isolation – Lack of support from friends and family can heighten feelings of paranoia and distress.
- Chronic stress – Prolonged exposure to financial struggles, work-related pressure, or caregiving responsibilities can increase symptom severity.

Since stress management is crucial for those at risk, therapy, mindfulness, and lifestyle adjustments can help reduce its impact.

2. Trauma and Early Life Experiences

Many individuals with schizophrenia have experienced trauma, particularly in early childhood. Trauma can disrupt brain

development, increasing vulnerability to psychotic symptoms later in life.
- Childhood abuse or neglect – Physical, emotional, or sexual abuse can contribute to long-term changes in brain function.
- Bullying and social rejection – Adolescents who experience severe bullying may develop paranoia or social withdrawal, both of which are linked to schizophrenia risk.
- Parental loss or instability – Growing up in an unpredictable or hostile environment can heighten stress responses, making the brain more prone to developing psychotic symptoms.

Studies show that individuals with schizophrenia often have higher rates of PTSD, suggesting a link between traumatic experiences and psychosis.

3. Substance Use and Psychosis

Certain substances can trigger psychotic episodes or worsen symptoms in those predisposed to schizophrenia. Some drugs interfere with dopamine regulation, which is already disrupted in schizophrenia.

- Cannabis – Heavy cannabis use, particularly at a young age, has been linked to an increased risk of schizophrenia. THC (the psychoactive compound in cannabis) affects dopamine levels, which can lead to paranoia and hallucinations.Stimulants (cocaine, amphetamines, methamphetamine) – These drugs increase dopamine activity, which can trigger psychotic symptoms, even in those without schizophrenia.
- Hallucinogens (LSD, psilocybin, ketamine) – These substances alter perception and can induce temporary psychotic states that may persist in individuals prone to schizophrenia.

- Alcohol and nicotine – While not direct causes, both substances are commonly used by individuals with schizophrenia, often as a way to self-medicate. However, they can contribute to worsening symptoms over time.
- Substance-induced psychosis can sometimes resolve after the drug is cleared from the system, but repeated use increases the risk of long-term psychotic disorders.

The Age of Onset: Why Schizophrenia Often Emerges in Late Teens or Early Adulthood

Schizophrenia typically develops between the late teens and early 30s, with most cases emerging in the late teens to mid-20s for men and the mid-20s to early 30s for women. It is rare for schizophrenia to appear in childhood or after the age of 40. But why does it tend to develop during this specific period of life? The answer lies in a combination of brain development, hormonal changes, and environmental factors.

1. Brain Development and Maturation
The human brain undergoes significant changes during adolescence and early adulthood. Many of these changes involve areas that are crucial for thought processing, emotional regulation, and perception of reality, which are all affected by schizophrenia.The prefrontal cortex (responsible for decision-making and reasoning) is still developing in the late teens and early 20s. If schizophrenia-related brain changes are already present, this period of development may bring symptoms to the surface.
- Synaptic pruning – During adolescence, the brain eliminates excess neural connections in a process called synaptic pruning. Some researchers believe that overactive pruning in schizophrenia

reduces important connections needed for clear thinking and reality perception.
- Dopamine system changes – The dopamine system, which plays a role in motivation, reward, and psychotic symptoms, is highly active in adolescence and early adulthood. Abnormal dopamine function may contribute to hallucinations and delusions.

2. Hormonal and Biological Factors
The transition from adolescence to adulthood is marked by major hormonal shifts, which can influence brain function and mental health.
- Increased stress hormone activity – The late teens and early 20s are a stressful period due to life changes, and stress can trigger or worsen schizophrenia symptoms.
- Sex hormones and gender differences – Estrogen is thought to have a

protective effect against schizophrenia, which may explain why women tend to develop the disorder slightly later than men. As estrogen levels fluctuate, symptoms may emerge.

3. Environmental Stressors and Life Transitions

Early adulthood is a time of significant life changes, such as leaving home, starting university or work, and forming new relationships. These events can act as triggers for schizophrenia symptoms in those who are already vulnerable.

- Increased independence and responsibility – The stress of handling finances, academics, and social expectations can be overwhelming.
- Substance use – Many young adults experiment with cannabis, alcohol, and other drugs, which can trigger psychosis or worsen symptoms.

- Social stress and isolation – This period often involves shifts in friendships, romantic relationships, and self-identity, all of which can contribute to emotional distress.

4. Genetic and Neurodevelopmental Factors
While schizophrenia is not fully determined by genetics, those with a family history of the disorder are at higher risk, and the late teens/early adulthood is often when genetic vulnerabilities begin to manifest. Some researchers also believe that early-life factors (such as birth complications, maternal infections, or childhood trauma) interact with brain development during adolescence to trigger schizophrenia.

Why Schizophrenia Rarely Appears in Childhood or Later Adulthood
Childhood-onset schizophrenia (before age 13) is extremely rare, likely because the brain has not yet reached the stage where schizophrenia-related changes take effect.

Late-onset schizophrenia (after age 40) is uncommon and often presents with fewer negative symptoms. Some researchers suggest that hormonal changes, late-life stress, or neurodegeneration may contribute to these cases.

CHAPTER 3

THE EXPERIENCE OF SCHIZOPHRENIA

Understanding Hallucinations: Voices, Visions, and Sensations

Hallucinations are one of the most well-known symptoms of schizophrenia. They occur when a person perceives things that are not actually there, affecting any of the five senses—hearing, sight, touch, smell, and taste. These experiences can feel incredibly real to the person experiencing them, making it difficult to distinguish between reality and hallucination.

1. Auditory Hallucinations: Hearing Voices and Sounds

Auditory hallucinations are the most common type in schizophrenia, affecting about 70% of individuals with the disorder. They typically involve:

- Hearing voices – These can be male or female, familiar or unknown, friendly or threatening.
- Multiple voices – Some people hear several voices at once, sometimes arguing or commenting on their actions.
- Command hallucinations – These voices may instruct the person to do certain things, which can be distressing or dangerous.
- Hearing sounds – Some report hearing whispers, clicks, buzzing, or footsteps when no one is there.

Brain imaging suggests that auditory hallucinations activate the same brain regions as real speech, which explains why they seem so real.

2. Visual Hallucinations: Seeing Things That Aren't There

Though less common than auditory hallucinations, visual hallucinations involve

seeing people, objects, or lights that do not exist. Examples include:
- Shadowy figures or people – Some individuals see faces, figures, or shapes that move around them.
- Flashes of light or colors – Some experience distorted colors, blurred vision, or glowing auras.
- Objects changing in shape or size – A person may see an object shifting, morphing, or pulsating unnaturally.

3. Tactile Hallucinations: Sensations on the Skin

Tactile (touch) hallucinations involve the sensation of being touched, grabbed, or moved, even when nothing is physically causing it. Examples include:
- Feeling bugs crawling on or under the skin – This can cause scratching or picking at the skin.
- Being pushed, pulled, or touched – Some feel invisible hands or forces acting on them.

- Temperature changes – Sudden sensations of heat, cold, or electrical shocks.

4. Olfactory and Gustatory Hallucinations: Smell and Taste Distortions

Though rare, some individuals experience hallucinations of smell or taste, which can be distressing.
- Smelling things that aren't there – A person may detect a rotting, burning, or chemical smell that others don't notice.
- Distorted taste – Food or drinks may taste spoiled, bitter, or metallic.

5. The Impact of Hallucinations

Hallucinations can be confusing, frightening, and isolating. Many people struggle to separate hallucinations from reality, which can lead to paranoia, distress, or unusual behaviors. Understanding and managing hallucinations is crucial for improving quality of life.

Delusions and Paranoia: When the Mind Creates Its Own Narrative

Delusions and paranoia are defining symptoms of schizophrenia, causing individuals to perceive a distorted version of reality. These beliefs are not just misunderstandings or exaggerated fears; they are deeply held convictions that persist even when presented with clear evidence to the contrary. Delusions can shape every aspect of a person's thoughts and actions, leading them to see threats, hidden messages, or extraordinary significance in everyday events.

1. What Are Delusions?
A delusion is a false belief that a person firmly believes despite logical proof against it. These beliefs can be bizarre (impossible things, like aliens controlling thoughts) or non-bizarre (things that could happen but aren't real, like being followed by the police without reason).

Common Types of Delusions in Schizophrenia:

- Persecutory Delusions (Paranoia) – The belief that someone is out to harm, spy on, or conspire against them. This is the most common type of delusion and can lead to extreme fear or isolation.
- Delusions of Grandeur – The belief that the person has extraordinary abilities, power, fame, or divine purpose. They may think they are a famous leader, a prophet, or have a mission to save the world.
- Delusions of Reference – The belief that random events, media, or people are sending secret messages meant specifically for them. Someone may think a TV show or news headline contains a hidden warning directed at them.
- Delusions of Control – The belief that external forces (aliens, government,

spirits) are controlling their thoughts, movements, or emotions. This can include thought insertion (believing thoughts are being placed in their mind) or thought broadcasting (believing others can hear their thoughts).
- Somatic Delusions – False beliefs about the body, such as thinking they have a serious disease, parasites under the skin, or that their organs have been replaced.

2. Paranoia: The Fear of Being Targeted
Paranoia is a specific type of delusion where a person believes they are being watched, persecuted, or controlled. This fear can make them highly suspicious of others, including family, friends, and doctors.A person may avoid phones, cameras, or technology, fearing they are being tracked.
They may believe strangers are following them or that the government is reading their

thoughts.Paranoia can lead to defensive or aggressive behavior, as the person feels the need to protect themselves from imagined threats.

3. How Delusions and Paranoia Affect Daily Life

These symptoms can be deeply isolating and disruptive. Someone experiencing delusions may:Withdraw from social connections, believing people are against them.Refuse treatment or medical care, thinking doctors are part of a conspiracy. Act in unusual ways, like covering mirrors, whispering to avoid being "overheard," or confronting strangers they believe are spying on them.

4. What Causes Delusions and Paranoia?

Delusions stem from abnormal brain activity, particularly involving dopamine, a chemical linked to perception and belief formation. Instead of filtering out irrelevant information, the brain connects random thoughts, events, or stimuli into a false but convincing narrative.

5. Managing and Treating Delusions
Medication (antipsychotics) can help regulate brain chemistry and reduce delusions. Cognitive Behavioral Therapy for Psychosis (CBTp) helps individuals examine their beliefs and develop coping strategies. Supportive relationships are key—people with delusions need understanding, not confrontation, as direct challenges to their beliefs can increase distress.

Cognitive and Emotional Struggles: Memory, Focus, and Motivation
Schizophrenia is often thought of in terms of hallucinations and delusions, but some of its most challenging symptoms involve cognitive and emotional difficulties. Many individuals with schizophrenia struggle with memory, focus, and motivation, making everyday tasks, social interactions, and

work responsibilities much harder. These challenges can persist even when hallucinations and delusions are under control, significantly impacting quality of life.

1. **Memory Problems: Forgetting and Confusion**
Schizophrenia can impair both short-term and long-term memory, leading to:
Forgetting conversations, appointments, or tasks soon after they happen.
Difficulty retaining new information, such as instructions or details from a book or movie.
Trouble recalling past experiences, especially when thoughts feel disorganized or clouded.These memory issues are linked to dysfunction in the prefrontal cortex, the brain region responsible for organizing and retrieving information.

2. Difficulty with Focus and Attention
People with schizophrenia often find it hard to concentrate or stay engaged in a task. This can manifest as:Easily getting

distracted by internal thoughts or external stimuli. Struggling to follow conversations because thoughts feel scattered.
Jumping between topics without completing one, leading to disorganized speech.
This lack of focus is partly due to imbalanced dopamine levels, which affect how the brain processes and prioritizes information.

3. Lack of Motivation (Avolition)
One of the most frustrating symptoms of schizophrenia is avolition, or a severe lack of motivation. This goes beyond laziness or procrastination—it feels like an inability to start or complete even simple tasks, such as:
- Getting dressed or showering

- Preparing meals or eating
- Engaging in hobbies or social activities

Avolition is caused by reduced dopamine function, making it difficult to feel reward or pleasure from activities that used to be enjoyable. As a result, individuals may withdraw from life, leading to social isolation and neglect of responsibilities.

4. Emotional Blunting: Feeling Disconnected
Schizophrenia can also dull emotions, making it hard to express or even feel feelings deeply. This can appear as:
- Flat affect – showing little facial expression or tone in speech.
- Reduced emotional responses – feeling disconnected from joy, sadness, or excitement.
- Difficulty forming emotional bonds – struggling to connect with family or friends.

5. Coping Strategies and Treatment
- While these challenges can be overwhelming, several strategies can help:

- Medication (antipsychotics) can reduce cognitive impairments by stabilizing dopamine levels.
- Cognitive Behavioral Therapy (CBT) can teach focus-building techniques and coping strategies.
- Structure and routines help maintain daily functioning, even when motivation is low.

Breaking tasks into small steps can make overwhelming activities more manageable.

CHAPTER 4

DIAGNOSIS AND TREATMENT OPTIONS

How Schizophrenia Is Diagnosed: Symptoms, Tests, and Evaluations

Schizophrenia is a complex mental health disorder, and diagnosing it requires a thorough evaluation by a psychiatrist or mental health professional. There is no single test for schizophrenia—instead, diagnosis is based on observing symptoms, ruling out other conditions, and assessing a person's thoughts, emotions, and behavior over time.

1. Recognizing the Symptoms
To be diagnosed with schizophrenia, a person must experience at least two of the following core symptoms for a significant portion of time over one month, with signs of disturbance lasting at least six months:

Hallucinations – Seeing, hearing, or sensing things that aren't there, such as voices or shadows.
- Delusions – Strongly held false beliefs, such as believing they are being watched, have special powers, or are receiving hidden messages.
- Disorganized Thinking – Speech may be jumbled, jumping between unrelated topics, or difficult to follow.
- Disorganized or Abnormal Behavior – Unpredictable actions, such as odd movements, lack of response, or inappropriate emotional reactions.
- Negative Symptoms – Lack of motivation, reduced speech, and emotional flatness.

At least one of the symptoms must be hallucinations, delusions, or disorganized speech for a schizophrenia diagnosis.

2. Psychological and Medical Evaluations

Diagnosing schizophrenia involves multiple assessments to rule out other conditions:
- Psychiatric Assessment
- A mental health professional will:
- Ask about thoughts, emotions, and behaviors – How symptoms affect daily life, relationships, and work.
- Assess perception of reality – Checking for hallucinations, delusions, or paranoia.
- Discuss family history – Schizophrenia has a genetic component, so family history can be a risk factor.

Medical Tests
Since some physical conditions can cause schizophrenia-like symptoms, doctors may perform tests such as:
- Blood tests and drug screenings – To rule out substance use, infections, or vitamin deficiencies.
- Brain scans (MRI or CT scan) – To check for structural abnormalities, tumors, or neurological disorders.

3. The DSM-5 Criteria
Psychiatrists use the Diagnostic and Statistical Manual of Mental Disorders (DSM-5) to officially diagnose schizophrenia. According to the DSM-5, symptoms must:
- Persist for at least six months, with at least one month of active symptoms.
- Significantly impair daily life, including work, relationships, or self-care.
- Not be explained by drug use or other medical conditions.

4. Differentiating Schizophrenia from Other Disorders
Schizophrenia shares symptoms with other conditions, so mental health professionals must distinguish it from:
- Bipolar disorder – Schizophrenia does not involve mood episodes as extreme as bipolar disorder.
- Schizoaffective disorder – Combines schizophrenia symptoms with mood disturbances (depression or mania).

- Substance-induced psychosis – Drug use can cause temporary psychotic symptoms.
- Severe depression with psychosis – Depression with hallucinations or delusions, but without other schizophrenia-related symptoms.

5. Early Diagnosis and Intervention
Schizophrenia typically emerges in the late teens or early adulthood, and early detection is crucial. The earlier a person receives treatment, the better their long-term outlook. Early warning signs may include:

Social withdrawal
- Decline in performance at school or work
- Unusual thinking patterns or paranoia
- Lack of motivation and emotional responses

Medications for Schizophrenia: Antipsychotics, Side Effects, and Benefits

Medication is a key part of schizophrenia treatment, helping to reduce symptoms such as hallucinations, delusions, and disorganized thinking. The primary type of medication used is antipsychotics, which work by balancing brain chemicals like dopamine and serotonin. While these medications can be highly effective, they also come with potential side effects that require careful management.

1. Types of Antipsychotic Medications
There are two main categories of antipsychotics:

First-Generation (Typical) Antipsychotics
These were developed in the 1950s and mainly block dopamine receptors to reduce psychotic symptoms. Examples include:
- Haloperidol (Haldol)
- Chlorpromazine (Thorazine)

- Fluphenazine (Prolixin)

Pros:
1. Effective at controlling hallucinations and delusions
2. Available in injectable forms for long-term use

Cons:
1. Higher risk of movement-related side effects (e.g., tremors, stiffness, restlessness)
2. May cause tardive dyskinesia (involuntary facial and body movements)

Second-Generation (Atypical) Antipsychotics
These newer medications affect both dopamine and serotonin, making them effective for both psychotic symptoms and mood regulation. Examples include:
- Risperidone (Risperdal)
- Olanzapine (Zyprexa)

- Quetiapine (Seroquel)
- Clozapine (Clozaril) – used for treatment-resistant schizophrenia

Pros:
1. Fewer movement-related side effects than first-generation drugs
2. May help with mood symptoms and cognitive function

Cons:
1. Higher risk of weight gain, diabetes, and metabolic issues
2. Some can cause sedation or drowsiness

2. Benefits of Antipsychotic Medication
   1. Reduces hallucinations and delusions – Helps individuals distinguish reality from psychosis.
   2. Improves thinking and focus – Allows for clearer thoughts and better communication.

3. Stabilizes mood and emotions – Can reduce anxiety, agitation, and severe mood swings.
4. Prevents relapse – Long-term medication use lowers the risk of future psychotic episodes.
5. Increases independence – Helps individuals function better in daily life, work, and relationships.

3. Common Side Effects

While effective, antipsychotics can cause a range of side effects that vary by individual and medication type. Some of the most common include:

Neurological Side Effects
- Drowsiness and fatigue – Some antipsychotics cause sedation, making it hard to stay alert.
- Tremors or muscle stiffness – Especially with first-generation drugs.
- Restlessness (Akathisia) – A feeling of needing to constantly move.

- Tardive Dyskinesia – Involuntary movements of the face, lips, and tongue (more common with long-term use of typical antipsychotics).

Metabolic Side Effects
- Weight gain – Many antipsychotics increase appetite, leading to obesity.
- Diabetes risk – Some drugs raise blood sugar levels, increasing diabetes risk.
- High cholesterol – Can contribute to heart disease over time.

Other Side Effects
1. Dry mouth or constipation
2. Dizziness or low blood pressure
3. Blurred vision
4. Hormonal changes (such as increased prolactin, which can affect menstrual cycles or cause breast enlargement in men)

4. Managing Side Effects

Doctors often start with low doses and adjust gradually to minimize side effects. Some strategies to help manage side effects include:
- Lifestyle changes – Regular exercise and a healthy diet can help with weight gain.
- Switching medications – If side effects are severe, a doctor may recommend a different drug.
- Adding supplements – Some people find that B vitamins, omega-3 fatty acids, or magnesium help with side effects.
- Regular check-ups – Monitoring blood sugar, cholesterol, and movement symptoms helps prevent long-term complications.

5. Long-Acting Injectable Medications (LAIs)
For individuals who struggle with taking daily pills, some antipsychotics are available as monthly or biweekly injections. These include:

- Paliperidone (Invega Sustenna)
- Risperidone (Risperdal Consta)
- Aripiprazole (Abilify Maintena)

Benefits of LAIs:
- Ensures consistent medication levels
- Reduces risk of relapse from missed doses
- Helpful for those who struggle with remembering to take daily pills

6. The Importance of Personalized Treatment

No single medication works for everyone, so finding the right one takes time. Many people try several different medications before finding the best fit. A combination of medication, therapy, and lifestyle changes provides the best outcome.

Therapy Options for Schizophrenia: CBT, Family Therapy, and Social Skills Training

While medication is essential for managing schizophrenia, therapy plays a crucial role in improving daily functioning, coping with symptoms, and rebuilding relationships. Different types of therapy help individuals develop insight into their condition, reduce distress, and improve communication and social interactions.

1. Cognitive Behavioral Therapy (CBT) for Schizophrenia

What it is:
CBT is a structured, goal-oriented therapy that helps individuals challenge and reframe distorted thoughts. It is one of the most effective non-medication treatments for reducing distress caused by hallucinations, delusions, and paranoia.

How it helps:
Reduces distress from hallucinations and delusions – While CBT does not eliminate hallucinations, it helps individuals understand that voices are not real and

develop coping strategies to ignore or manage them.
1. Challenges irrational beliefs – CBT helps patients recognize when delusions are unrealistic and teaches them to question the evidence supporting these beliefs.
2. Improves emotional regulation – Helps with managing anxiety, stress, and depression, which often accompany schizophrenia.
3. Teaches coping skills – Individuals learn strategies such as distraction techniques, grounding exercises, and problem-solving methods to reduce distress.

Example technique:
If a person believes they are being watched, the therapist might ask:
- "What evidence do you have for this belief?"
- "Has this happened before? If so, what was the actual outcome?"

- "Could there be another explanation?"

2. Family Therapy: Supporting Loved Ones

What it is:
Schizophrenia affects not only the individual but also their family. Family therapy helps educate, support, and improve communication between the person with schizophrenia and their loved ones.

How it helps:
Reduces family stress and conflict – Family members learn how to support without enabling and avoid unhelpful responses.
- Teaches communication skills – Families learn how to talk openly and calmly without escalating distress.
- Helps prevent relapse – A supportive home environment reduces the risk of relapse and hospitalization.
- Encourages problem-solving – Families develop practical ways to

handle crises, medication management, and daily challenges.

Example technique:
Teaching active listening to improve communication and reduce misunderstandings.
Role-playing how to respond when a loved one is experiencing paranoia or hallucinations without reinforcing their delusions.

3. Social Skills Training: Rebuilding Daily Functioning

What it is:
Social skills training focuses on helping individuals develop the skills needed for everyday interactions, work, and independent living.

How it helps:
Improves verbal and nonverbal communication – Helps individuals learn

how to hold conversations, interpret body language, and express themselves clearly.
- Teaches problem-solving for real-life situations – Covers skills like job interviews, handling public spaces, and making friends.
- Enhances independence – Training includes self-care, budgeting, and managing responsibilities.
- Boosts confidence and reduces social isolation – Helps individuals feel more comfortable in social settings.

Example technique:
- Role-playing social scenarios – Practicing introductions, making eye contact, and responding appropriately in conversations.
- Using video feedback – Reviewing recorded interactions to identify and improve social cues.

4. Other Therapy Approaches

- Art or Music Therapy – Helps with self-expression and emotional regulation.
- Mindfulness and Relaxation Training – Reduces stress and anxiety, improving overall well-being.
- Vocational Rehabilitation – Helps individuals find and maintain jobs by teaching workplace skills and coping strategies.

Hospitalization and Crisis Management in Schizophrenia

Schizophrenia is a complex mental health condition that can sometimes lead to crises requiring immediate intervention and hospitalization. Managing these crises effectively can prevent harm, stabilize symptoms, and ensure long-term well-being. Understanding when hospitalization is necessary and how crisis management works can help individuals, families, and caregivers navigate difficult situations.

1. When is Hospitalization Necessary?
Hospitalization is considered when a person with schizophrenia is experiencing:
- Severe psychotic episodes – If hallucinations, delusions, or paranoia make it impossible to function safely.
- Danger to self or others – If a person is suicidal, aggressive, or at risk of harming others, immediate intervention is required.
- Inability to care for oneself – If a person is not eating, drinking, or maintaining hygiene, they may need hospital care.
- Medication crisis – If severe side effects or stopping medication suddenly leads to relapse or dangerous withdrawal symptoms.
- Substance use complications – If drug or alcohol use worsens symptoms and increases risky behavior.

2. Types of Hospitalization

- Voluntary Hospitalization – The individual agrees to treatment and admits themselves for stabilization.
- Involuntary Hospitalization – If someone is unable to recognize their condition or is a danger to themselves or others, they may be admitted under mental health laws (such as the Mental Health Act in the UK or involuntary commitment laws in the US).
- Short-Term vs. Long-Term Care – Some hospital stays are a few days to stabilize symptoms, while others may last weeks or months for deeper treatment and medication adjustments.

3. Crisis Management Strategies
Crisis situations can often be prevented or de-escalated with proper planning. Here's how crisis management works:

For Individuals with Schizophrenia

- Recognizing warning signs – Understanding early symptoms like increased paranoia, withdrawal, or skipping medication can help seek help before a crisis escalates.
- Having a crisis plan – Keeping a written plan with emergency contacts, preferred hospitals, and medication details.
- Using grounding techniques – Practicing deep breathing, focusing on physical sensations, or listening to calming music can help during distressing moments.
- Reaching out for help – Calling a trusted friend, family member, therapist, or crisis hotline when feeling overwhelmed.

For Families and Caregivers
- Staying calm and patient – Avoid arguing about delusions or hallucinations; instead, offer reassurance and support.

- Encouraging professional help – Suggest seeing a doctor or crisis team before the situation worsens.
- Avoiding confrontation – Speak in a calm, non-threatening tone and give the person space if they are agitated.
- Knowing emergency contacts – Having the nearest hospital, mental health crisis team, and helplines readily available.

4. After Hospitalization: Recovery and Support
- Hospitalization is just the first step—ongoing care is essential for long-term stability. After discharge, key steps include:
- Medication adherence – Ensuring medications are taken as prescribed to prevent relapse.
- Therapy and counseling – Engaging in CBT, social skills training, or family therapy.

- Community support – Joining peer support groups, mental health programs, or rehabilitation services.
- Lifestyle adjustments – Encouraging a healthy routine, good nutrition, sleep, and stress management.

CHAPTER 5

LIVING WITH SCHIZOPHRENIA

Coping Strategies for Daily Life with Schizophrenia

Living with schizophrenia presents daily challenges, but with the right coping strategies, individuals can manage symptoms, improve well-being, and maintain independence. A combination of self-care, structured routines, and support systems can make everyday life more manageable.

1. Managing Symptoms
    - Medication Adherence – Taking medication as prescribed is essential for stabilizing symptoms and preventing relapse. Setting reminders, using pill organizers, or having a trusted person check in can help.

- Recognizing Triggers – Identifying what worsens symptoms (e.g., stress, isolation, sleep deprivation) can help in avoiding or managing these triggers.
- Reality-Checking Techniques – If experiencing hallucinations or delusions, asking "Is there evidence to support this?" or talking to a trusted person can help separate reality from symptoms.

2. Building a Healthy Routine
    - Structured Daily Schedule – Following a consistent routine for meals, sleep, work, and activities provides stability and reduces uncertainty.
    - Regular Sleep Patterns – Aiming for 7-9 hours of sleep can help regulate mood and prevent episodes of psychosis.
    - Healthy Diet and Exercise – Eating nutritious foods and engaging in light

exercise (like walking or yoga) supports mental and physical health.

3. Coping with Stress and Emotions
   - Mindfulness and Relaxation Techniques – Practices like deep breathing, meditation, and progressive muscle relaxation help in reducing anxiety and grounding reality.
   - Creative Outlets – Activities like art, music, journaling, or gardening can provide emotional relief and a sense of accomplishment.
   - Breaking Tasks into Small Steps – Managing daily responsibilities by focusing on one task at a time prevents feeling overwhelmed.

4. Strengthening Social Support
   1. Staying Connected – Maintaining relationships with family, friends, or support groups prevents isolation and offers emotional support.

2. Attending Therapy or Support Groups – Regular participation in CBT, group therapy, or schizophrenia support communities provides guidance and encouragement.
3. Practicing Communication Skills – Using role-playing or social skills training can help navigate social interactions more effectively.

5. Managing Work and Responsibilities
   1. Finding Suitable Work or Volunteering – Jobs with flexible schedules, low stress, and supportive environments can be beneficial. Vocational rehabilitation services can help with job placement.
   2. Using Reminders and Lists – Writing down appointments, tasks, and reminders helps with memory and focus.
   3. Asking for Accommodations – At work or school, requesting flexible

deadlines, quiet spaces, or additional support can improve performance.

6. Seeking Help When Needed
    1. Recognizing Early Warning Signs – Symptoms like increased paranoia, withdrawal, or trouble thinking clearly may indicate a need for help.
    2. Reaching Out to a Trusted Person – Talking to a therapist, doctor, or family member when feeling overwhelmed can prevent a crisis.
    3. Having a Crisis Plan – Keeping emergency contacts, medication details, and a list of calming strategies readily available can help in difficult moments.

Managing Stress and Triggers in Schizophrenia

Stress is a significant factor in schizophrenia, as it can worsen symptoms, trigger episodes, or lead to relapse. Identifying and managing stressors effectively can help individuals maintain stability and improve overall well-being.

1. Identifying Personal Triggers
Schizophrenia triggers vary from person to person, but common ones include:
1. Stressful Life Events – Job loss, financial issues, or relationship conflicts.
2. Social Isolation – Loneliness or lack of support can worsen symptoms.
3. Lack of Sleep – Sleep disturbances can increase confusion and paranoia.
4. Substance Use – Alcohol, drugs, and even excessive caffeine can trigger psychotic episodes.
5. Sensory Overload – Crowded places, loud noises, or bright lights may be overwhelming.
6. Medication Changes – Skipping doses or stopping medication suddenly can lead to relapse.

Recognizing these triggers early allows for preventative action before they escalate into a crisis.

2. Stress Management Techniques
    1. Structured Routine – A predictable daily schedule reduces uncertainty and provides stability.
    2. Relaxation Techniques – Deep breathing, meditation, and progressive muscle relaxation can calm the nervous system.
    3. Physical Activity – Walking, yoga, or stretching can reduce stress and improve mental clarity.
    4. Creative Outlets – Art, music, journaling, or hobbies can serve as a healthy distraction.
    5. Time Management – Breaking tasks into smaller steps prevents feeling overwhelmed.

3. Developing Healthy Coping Strategies

1. Reality-Checking – If experiencing paranoia or delusions, talking to a trusted person or writing down logical counterpoints can help ground reality.
2. Social Support – Engaging with friends, family, or support groups reduces stress and provides reassurance.
3. Self-Compassion – Avoiding self-criticism and recognizing that progress takes time.
4. Setting Boundaries – Avoiding stressful environments or negative relationships that may worsen symptoms.

4. Preparing for High-Stress Situations
   1. Have a Crisis Plan – Keeping emergency contacts, medication details, and calming strategies written down.
   2. Use Grounding Techniques – Engaging the senses (e.g., holding an object, listening to music, focusing on

breathing) can help in distressing moments.
3. Avoiding Overstimulation – Limiting exposure to loud environments, large crowds, or excessive screen time.

5. Seeking Professional Help
Therapy (CBT or Stress Management Therapy) – Learning techniques to reframe negative thoughts and manage anxiety.
- Medication Adjustments – If stress is leading to increased symptoms, consulting a doctor about possible medication changes.
- Regular Check-Ins with Mental Health Professionals – Ongoing support helps prevent small stressors from turning into larger problems.

Building a Support Network: Family, Friends, and Professionals
Living with schizophrenia can be challenging, but a strong support network can make a significant difference in

managing symptoms, reducing isolation, and improving overall well-being. A combination of family, friends, mental health professionals, and support groups provides both emotional and practical help.

1. The Role of Family in Support
Family members can be a crucial source of stability for individuals with schizophrenia. They provide:
1. Emotional support – Encouragement, patience, and reassurance during difficult times.
2. Practical help – Assisting with daily responsibilities like appointments, medication reminders, and meals.
3. Education and advocacy – Learning about schizophrenia to better understand symptoms and challenges.
4. Crisis intervention – Recognizing warning signs of relapse and seeking professional help if needed.

Tips for Strengthening Family Support:
1. Encourage open communication – Creating a safe space to express feelings without judgment.
2. Set realistic expectations – Understanding that progress takes time and setbacks may happen.
3. Practice patience and empathy – Schizophrenia is not a choice; symptoms can be overwhelming.
4. Join family support groups – Organizations like NAMI (National Alliance on Mental Illness) offer education and guidance for loved ones.

2. Friends as a Social Safety Net
Friends can offer companionship, encouragement, and a sense of normalcy in everyday life. Having a social support system helps:
1. Reduce loneliness and isolation – Social interactions improve mood and emotional well-being.

2. Provide a distraction from symptoms – Engaging in hobbies, activities, or casual conversations can help.
3. Boost confidence and self-worth – Positive social experiences reinforce a sense of belonging.

How to Strengthen Friendships:
1. Be honest about your condition – Educate close friends about schizophrenia so they can better understand and support you.
2. Stay connected in ways that feel comfortable – Texting, calling, or meeting in small groups if large gatherings feel overwhelming.
3. Find shared activities – Hobbies, exercise, or creative projects can strengthen friendships without pressure.

3. The Importance of Mental Health Professionals

A team of mental health professionals plays a vital role in treatment and stability:
- Psychiatrists – Manage medications and monitor symptoms.
- Therapists (CBT, DBT, or social skills training) – Help with coping strategies, emotional regulation, and reality testing.
- Case managers or social workers – Assist with housing, employment, and accessing support services.
- Peer support specialists – Individuals who have lived with schizophrenia and can provide mentorship and understanding.

How to Make the Most of Professional Support:
- Keep regular appointments – Consistency helps in tracking progress and preventing relapses.
- Be honest about symptoms – Transparency helps in adjusting treatment plans effectively.

- Ask about additional resources – Support programs, job assistance, and therapy groups can enhance well-being.

4. Support Groups and Community Resources

Joining schizophrenia support groups offers a sense of belonging and shared understanding. These groups can be:
- In-person or online – Local mental health centers and platforms like Reddit or Facebook host communities.
- Led by professionals or peers – Some are run by therapists, while others are peer-led for shared experiences.
- Focused on different needs – Groups exist for young adults, families, relapse prevention, and life skills training.

Popular Support Organizations:

National Alliance on Mental Illness (NAMI) – Offers education, peer support, and advocacy.
- Schizophrenia and Related Disorders Alliance of America (SARDAA) – Provides support groups and information.
- Hearing Voices Network – Specializes in supporting those experiencing auditory hallucinations.

5. Setting Boundaries and Maintaining Balance

While a support network is crucial, it's also important to:
1. Set boundaries with family and friends – Avoid toxic relationships or over-reliance that may cause stress.
2. Balance independence and support – Accept help when needed, but also work towards personal growth.
3. Know when to seek help – If symptoms worsen, reach out to a professional or trusted person.

Overcoming Stigma and Self-Doubt in Schizophrenia

Schizophrenia is one of the most misunderstood mental health conditions, often surrounded by stigma, fear, and misinformation. This can lead to self-doubt, shame, and reluctance to seek help. However, with education, self-acceptance, and strong support, individuals with schizophrenia can challenge stigma, build confidence, and live fulfilling lives.

1. Understanding Stigma: Where It Comes From

Stigma surrounding schizophrenia often comes from:

    a. Media Misrepresentation – Movies and TV shows often portray people with schizophrenia as dangerous or out of control, which is far from reality.

    b. Lack of Public Awareness – Many people don't understand that schizophrenia is a medical condition, not a character flaw.

c. Social Avoidance – Fear and misunderstanding may cause friends, family, or employers to treat someone differently.
   d. Internalized Stigma – Negative societal attitudes can lead individuals to believe harmful stereotypes about themselves, increasing feelings of worthlessness.

2. Breaking the Cycle of Self-Doubt
People with schizophrenia may struggle with self-doubt due to symptoms like delusions, hallucinations, or cognitive difficulties. This can lead to:
   a. Feeling like they are a burden to others.
   b. Believing they will never achieve their goals.
   c. Avoiding social interactions due to fear of judgment.

To combat self-doubt:

I. Recognize that schizophrenia does not define you – It is a medical condition, not your identity.
II. Focus on strengths and achievements – Celebrate small victories, whether it's managing symptoms, keeping a routine, or completing a personal goal.
III. Challenge negative thoughts – Cognitive Behavioral Therapy (CBT) can help replace self-critical thoughts with positive, realistic ones.
IV. Surround yourself with supportive people – Having family, friends, and mental health professionals who believe in you can boost confidence.

3. Educating Others: Fighting Stigma with Knowledge

One of the best ways to overcome stigma is through education and advocacy:
I. Share your story – If comfortable, talking about personal experiences can help others understand schizophrenia better.

II. Correct misinformation – When people make incorrect assumptions, calmly provide facts.
III. Encourage open conversations – Talking about mental health reduces fear and misunderstanding.

Organizations like NAMI (National Alliance on Mental Illness) and SARDAA (Schizophrenia and Related Disorders Alliance of America) offer resources to educate the public and fight stigma.

4. Finding Strength in Community
Join peer support groups – Being around others who understand your experience can help combat feelings of isolation.
I. Connect with advocates – There are many individuals openly living with schizophrenia who are working to change perceptions.
II. Seek professional support – Therapy can help develop coping strategies to manage stigma and self-doubt.

5. Practicing Self-Compassion and Resilience
Remind yourself that progress is not linear – There will be good days and bad days, but that does not define your worth.
   I. Engage in self-care – Exercise, hobbies, mindfulness, and healthy routines can boost confidence.
   II. Set realistic goals – Accomplishing small, manageable goals helps build self-esteem.

CHAPTER 6

HOPE, RECOVERY, AND THE FUTURE

Can Schizophrenia Be Cured? Understanding Long-Term Management
Schizophrenia is a chronic mental health condition, meaning there is no known cure. However, with the right treatment, support, and self-care strategies, many people with schizophrenia can manage their symptoms effectively and lead fulfilling, independent lives.

1. Why Isn't There a Cure?
Schizophrenia is a complex disorder that affects brain structure, neurotransmitters, and cognitive function. Researchers have yet to discover a single cause, making a complete cure difficult. However, advancements in treatment allow for better

symptom control and improved quality of life.

2. Long-Term Management Strategies
While schizophrenia cannot be cured, it can be successfully managed through:

A. Medication (Antipsychotics)
Reduces symptoms like hallucinations, delusions, and paranoia.

Two main types:
- Typical antipsychotics (older medications) – Effective but may have more side effects.
- Atypical antipsychotics (newer medications) – Fewer movement-related side effects but may cause weight gain or metabolic issues.
- Consistency is key – Stopping medication abruptly can lead to relapse.

B. Therapy and Counseling
Cognitive Behavioral Therapy (CBT) – Helps challenge delusions, manage paranoia, and improve coping skills.
- Family Therapy – Educates loved ones and improves communication.
- Social Skills Training – Helps with relationships, work, and daily interactions.

C. Lifestyle and Self-Care
- Healthy Diet & Exercise – Reduces stress, improves brain function, and counters medication side effects.
- Sleep and Routine – Regular schedules help stabilize mood and thinking.
- Stress Management – Mindfulness, meditation, and hobbies can improve emotional well-being.

D. Social and Community Support

- Support groups – Connecting with others who understand the condition reduces isolation.
- Case management & housing programs – Assist with employment, daily tasks, and independent living.

3. Can People with Schizophrenia Recover?
Yes! While there is no cure, many people achieve long-term stability with the right treatment. Recovery is different for everyone:
1. Some may experience only one episode and never relapse.
2. Others may have occasional flare-ups but manage well with medication and therapy.
3. Some may require ongoing support but can still live meaningful lives.

4. Hope for the Future: Advancements in Research

Scientists are working on:

I. Better medications with fewer side effects.
II. New brain stimulation therapies to improve symptoms.
III. Personalized treatments based on genetics and brain scans.

Diet and Schizophrenia: Foods That Support Mental Health

While there is no specific diet that can cure schizophrenia, nutrition plays a vital role in managing symptoms, improving brain function, and reducing side effects of medication. A balanced, nutrient-rich diet can help stabilize mood, support cognitive function, and enhance overall well-being.

1. Key Nutrients for Brain Health
A. Omega-3 Fatty Acids – Supports brain function and reduces inflammation
Found in: Fatty fish (salmon, sardines, mackerel), flaxseeds, chia seeds, walnuts

Studies suggest omega-3s may help reduce symptoms of schizophrenia, particularly in the early stages.

B. Antioxidants – Protects brain cells from oxidative stress
Found in: Berries, spinach, kale, dark chocolate, green tea
Schizophrenia is linked to increased oxidative stress, which may contribute to symptoms like memory issues and cognitive decline.

C. B Vitamins (Especially B6, B9, and B12) – Helps with mood and brain function
Found in: Leafy greens, eggs, dairy, fish, fortified cereals, lentils
Low levels of B vitamins have been associated with higher rates of schizophrenia symptoms.

D. Vitamin D – Important for mental health and immune function

Found in: Sunlight, fortified dairy, fatty fish, mushrooms
Many people with schizophrenia have low vitamin D levels, which can contribute to mood disturbances.

E. Magnesium and Zinc – Helps regulate brain chemistry and neurotransmitters
Magnesium sources: Nuts, seeds, whole grains, dark leafy greens
Zinc sources: Pumpkin seeds, chickpeas, red meat, shellfish
Studies suggest these minerals may improve cognitive function and emotional stability.

2. Foods to Include in a Schizophrenia-Friendly Diet
   I.   Whole Foods – Focus on unprocessed, natural foods rather than highly processed meals.
   II. Lean Proteins – Fish, chicken, turkey, eggs, and plant-based proteins help with brain function.

III. Fermented Foods – Yogurt, kefir, kimchi, and sauerkraut support gut health, which is linked to mental health.
IV. Complex Carbohydrates – Whole grains, quinoa, brown rice, and sweet potatoes provide steady energy and prevent blood sugar spikes, which can affect mood.
V. Healthy Fats – Avocados, olive oil, nuts, and seeds help with brain function and inflammation control.

3. Foods to Avoid or Limit

A. Processed and Sugary Foods
Why? High sugar intake can cause blood sugar spikes, leading to mood instability.
Examples: Candy, soda, white bread, fast food.

B. Artificial Additives and Preservatives

Why? Some studies suggest that certain food additives may worsen symptoms in sensitive individuals.
Examples: Processed meats, instant noodles, artificial sweeteners.

C. Caffeine and Stimulants
Why? Too much caffeine can increase anxiety and paranoia, worsening schizophrenia symptoms.
Examples: Energy drinks, excessive coffee, strong teas.

D. Excessive Alcohol and Substance Use
Why? Alcohol and drugs can interfere with medication and worsen mental health symptoms.

4. The Gut-Brain Connection
Recent research suggests a link between gut health and schizophrenia. A healthy gut microbiome may help regulate brain function and mental health. Eating probiotic-rich foods (like yogurt and sauerkraut) and fiber-

rich foods (like vegetables and legumes) can support gut health.

5. Hydration Matters
Drinking plenty of water prevents dehydration, which can lead to confusion, fatigue, and mood swings. Aim for at least 6-8 glasses per day.

Finding Meaning and Hope Beyond the Diagnosis
A schizophrenia diagnosis can feel overwhelming, bringing uncertainty, fear, and self-doubt. However, a diagnosis does not define a person. Many individuals with schizophrenia find ways to live fulfilling lives, build meaningful relationships, and pursue their passions. With the right support, treatment, and mindset, hope and purpose are always within reach.
1. Accepting the Diagnosis: The First Step Toward Growth
   I. It's natural to feel anger, sadness, or denial, but accepting the diagnosis is

      the first step toward taking control of one's life.
- II. Understanding schizophrenia as a manageable condition, rather than a life sentence, can shift perspective and open doors to possibilities.
- III. Many successful individuals, including writers, artists, and advocates, live with schizophrenia and use their experiences to inspire others.

2. Redefining Identity Beyond the Illness
A diagnosis is not a label—it is just one part of a person's story.
Focusing on strengths, talents, and passions can help create a strong sense of self.Exploring hobbies, education, and meaningful work provides purpose beyond the illness.

3. Building a Supportive and Understanding Community
- I. Surrounding oneself with supportive friends, family, and mental health

professionals makes a huge difference.
II. Connecting with support groups (in-person or online) helps reduce isolation and offers hope through shared experiences.
III. Advocating for mental health awareness can empower individuals to use their experiences to educate and inspire others.

4. Setting Realistic Goals and Celebrating Progress
I. Small steps lead to big changes—whether it's managing symptoms, developing routines, or pursuing dreams.
II. Tracking progress and celebrating achievements boosts confidence and motivation.
III. Every challenge overcome is a reminder of inner strength and resilience.

5. Finding Purpose Through Creativity and Expression
   I. Many people with schizophrenia find healing through art, music, writing, or spirituality.
   II. Creative expression can help process emotions, reduce stress, and bring joy.
   III. Sharing one's story can help others feel less alone and reduce stigma around mental health.

6. Embracing Hope for the Future
   I. New treatments and therapies continue to improve quality of life for those with schizophrenia.
   II. Many individuals find love, success, and happiness, despite their diagnosis.
   III. Hope comes from recognizing that life is not defined by limitations, but by the strength to keep moving forward.

Made in the USA
Monee, IL
27 April 2025